Valentine's Day

Kathryn A. Imler

Heinemann Library
Chicago, Illinois

H HEINEMANN-RAINTREE

TO ORDER:

☎ Phone Customer Service **888-454-2279**

🖥 Visit **www.heinemannraintree.com** to browse our catalog and order online.

©2003, 2008 Heinemann-Raintree
a division of Pearson Education Limited
Chicago, Illinois

Editorial: Rebecca Rissman
Design: Kimberly R. Miracle and Tony Miracle
Picture Research: Kathy Creech and Tracy Cummins
Production: Duncan Gilbert

Originated by Chroma Graphics (Overseas) Pte. Ltd
Printed and bound in China by South China Printing Co. Ltd.
The paper used to print this book comes from sustainable resources.

ISBN-13: 978-1-4329-1045-7 (hc)
ISBN-10: 1-4329-1045-0 (hc)
ISBN-13: 978-1-4329-1053-2 (pb)
ISBN-10: 1-4329-1053-1 (pb)

12 11 10 09 08
10 9 8 7 6 5 4 3 2 1

Library of Congress Cataloging-in-Publication Data
Imler, Kathryn A., 1950-
    Valentine's Day / Katheryn Imler
       p-cm. – (Holiday histories)
Summary: Presents background information on the origins and traditions of customs related to the celebration of St. Valentine's Day.
Includes bibliographical references and index.
    ISBN: 978-1-4329-1045-7 (HC) 978-1-4329-1053-2 (PB)
1. Valentine's Day—Juvenile literature. [1. Valentine's Day.
2. Holidays] I. Title. II. Series.
 GT4925.155 2003
394.2618—dc22
                                    2003007888

Acknowledgments
The author and publishers are grateful to the following for permission to reproduce copyright material: **p.4** ©James and James Photography/Jupiter Images; **p.5** ©Jose Luis Pelaez Inc/Getty Images; **pp.6, 7, 9, 11, 13, 15, 16** ©Hulton Archive/Getty Images; **p.10** ©akg images-London; **pp. 12, 17, 20, 21** ©North Wind Picture Archive; **P. 14** ©Richard Cummins/Corbis; **p.18** ©Mary Evans Picture Library; **p.19T** ©Bettmann/Corbis; **p.19B** ©KJ Historical/Corbis; **p.22, 23** ©American Antiquarian Society; **p.24** ©William Hart/Stone/Getty Images; **p.25** ©Ariel Skelley/Getty Images; **p.26** ©Burke/Triolo Productions/Food Pix/Getty Images; **p.27** ©The Bridgeman Art Library/Getty Images; **p.28** ©Rommel/Masterfile; **p.29** ©Jose Luis Pelaez, Inc./Corbis;

Cover photograph reproduced with the permission of ©Corbis/Jupiterimages/Brand X

Every effort has been made to contact copyright holders of any material reproduced in this book. Any omissions will be rectified in subsequent printings if notice is given to the publisher.

Disclaimer
All the Internet addresses (URLs) given in this book were valid at the time of going to press. However, due to the dynamic nature of the Internet, some addresses may have changed, or sites may have changed or ceased to exist since publication. While the author and publisher regret any inconvenience this may cause readers, no responsibility for any such changes can be accepted by either the author or the publisher.

Contents

Some words are shown in bold, **like this**. You can find out what they mean by looking in the glossary.

A Holiday About Love

Red hearts hang everywhere. People bake cookies and dust them with red sprinkles. Stickers and colored candy hearts say, "I love you."

It is Valentine's Day. People send pretty cards. They give flowers and candy to special friends. It is a special time when we can tell people how much we care for them. But where did this special day come from?

A Roman Festival

This is a drawing of a Roman chariot race.

Many people believe Valentine's Day began as
a Roman **festival**. In ancient Rome, the first day
of spring was February 15. The Romans held a
festival to celebrate this. They sang songs, danced
and had races.

This drawing shows Roman children playing at a festival.

The day before the festival, girls put their names on slips of paper. Boys drew the name of a girl from a bowl. She was his playmate for the festival. Sometimes they fell in love.

A Man Named Valentine

A Catholic **priest** lived in Rome at this same time. His name was Valentine. Some people believe Valentine went against the emperor's law. They say he secretly married young couples in love.

This picture shows Valentine being arrested.

Soon Emperor Claudius found out. He **arrested** Valentine and put him in jail. He had Valentine put to death on February 14.

Early Customs

Over time, other countries started to celebrate Valentine's Day. Each one had its own **customs**. In France, fancy dances were held for young men and women.

In Italy, couples often walked through gardens together. Men read love poems to the ladies. Soft music was part of the celebration, too.

Other Gifts

There are other ways to say, "Happy Valentine's Day."
Anything shaped like a heart is a good gift. Some
people bake cookies.

Sweet treats like candy are also nice. Some people give flowers. Red roses are very special.